DEADLY 60

>>>>> Factbook:
Fish, Squid and Jellyfish

Look out for the
other DEADLY books:

OUT NOW :

Deadly Factbook: Mammals
Deadly Factbook Minibeasts: Insects and Spiders
Deadly Factbook: Reptiles and Amphibians
Deadly Factbook: Bizarre Beasts

Deadly Activity Book
Deadly Brain Teasers
Deadly Top 10 Activity Book
Deadly Doodle Book 1, 2 and 3
Deadly Diaries
Deadly Detectives

Some **CATFISH** live in
muddy rivers or underwater caves where
it can be hard to find prey. To help, a catfish has
long whiskers called barbels around its mouth.
These are covered with thousands of tiny nerve
endings and receptors so the fish knows just
what's around, even in total darkness.

Catfish also have more than
100,000 taste buds on their body.

Fish don't have ears
on the outside of the body
that you can see, but they
can hear sounds and this may help them
find prey. Sound waves travel through
a fish's body to the ears inside its body.

Bony fish also have a special sense
called the lateral line. This is made up of
a series of specialised cells along each side
of the fish's body. These pick up the slightest
vibrations in the water and help the fish find
its way around as well as locate prey.

BARRACUDAS are the wolves of the sea. These long, slender predatory fish often hunt in shoals and can chop their prey in half with their terrifyingly sharp teeth.

The **GREAT WHITE SHARK**

has as many as 300 teeth, arranged in rows in its jaws. It uses the teeth in the first two rows for tearing flesh from its prey. The teeth in the other rows are there ready to move into place if the shark loses any teeth as it feeds. That way it is never without a full set of teeth.

Because sharks' teeth are shed constantly through life, and are made of hard material, teeth from great whites and their ancestors are some of the most frequently found fossils. From these fossils, scientists now believe such sharks were once as big as sperm whales!

BULL SHARKS grow to 3.5 metres long. They have large bulky heads and are known to be among the most aggressive of all sharks. Although they spend most of their time in shallow coastal waters, bull sharks are known to swim up into rivers, such as the Amazon.

Sharks may be scary, but shark attacks on humans are actually very rare. Every year sharks attack only about 50-75 people and there may be 8 deaths. Many more people are killed by bee stings – and by being struck by lightning.

One of the most impressive predatory fish in British seas is the

CONGER EEL

which can grow up to 3 metres long.

The conger usually hunts by lurking in a hole or crevice and watching for prey to swim by. When something comes within reach, the conger snatches it, or may just suck it down its throat. If the prey is too large to swallow whole, the conger takes hold of its catch and spins itself round to twist out a chunk of flesh.

The **HUMBOLDT SQUID** spends the day in deep water but comes up to surface waters at night to feed on fish, shrimp and other creatures. It seizes prey with its strong arms, which are lined with barbed suckers, and pulls it to its mouth. It then tears the prey apart with its sharp beak. Like other squid, the Humboldt can change colour with its mood – it turns bright red when angry!

Did you know that some fish can make electricity in their own bodies? Most powerful is the

ELECTRIC EEL.

This fish grows to 2.5 metres long and can deliver a burst of electricity of up to 600 volts – enough to stun and even kill a person. Despite its name, this is not a true eel but a knifefish, one of a group of elongated, knife-shaped fish that are more closely related to catfish than eels.

The electric eel uses its electric charge to attack prey and to defend itself. It's also believed to use its electric powers to navigate, like a kind of natural radar.

The **MANTIS SHRIMP**
has one of the fastest punches of
any animal on Earth. This creature,
which is anything from 2-30
centimetres long depending
on the species,
lies in wait for prey
in a hole in the sea bed.

When the shrimp spots
something, it zooms
out and stuns the prey
with a powerful blow. This is strong
enough to smash through the shells of creatures
such as snails, crabs and barnacles.

The mantis shrimp's club-like
arms move at 80 kilometres an hour
and accelerate faster than a bullet.

The **PIKE** hunts by stealth.
The biggest predatory fish
in British rivers,
the pike can lurk
almost motionless
in the water as it
watches for prey.
When a likely
victim comes close, the pike darts forward to
grab hold of the prey in its sharp spiky teeth.

Other fish – even smaller pike –
are the pike's main food.
It also eats frogs, water birds and
small mammals such as voles.

Pike can grow up to 1.5 metres long.
Females are larger than males.

BIZARRE BODIES

DEADLY

Chapter 6

The **HAMMERHEAD SHARK** has one of the strangest heads of any fish. Its eyes and nostrils are at each end of the hammer shape and this arrangement is thought to make its senses of sight and smell extra efficient.

This arrangement may also increase the efficiency of the special sensing organs that detect electrical activity. These help the shark find prey such as stingray hidden in the sand on the sea bed.

With its long broad snout and jaws
studded with 2 rows of sharp teeth, the

ALLIGATOR GAR

looks just like a crocodile at the front end,
but the rest of its body is clearly a fish.

This fierce predator grows up to 3 metres long
and lives in rivers in the southeastern USA.
While most of its diet is made up of other fish,
it also catches birds and small mammals that
wander close to the riverbank.

The
STINGRAY

has a flattened body, side fins and a long whiplike tail and looks more like a kite than a fish. Its eyes are on the top of its head but the mouth and nostrils are on its underside. The long tail has a sharp spine with serrated edges at its base. This barb is linked to a venom gland and is used by the stingray to defend itself if threatened – or stepped on by an unwary diver!

The **THRESHER SHARK** grows to 6 metres long, nearly 3 metres of which is the long upper tail fin.

The thresher's tail is actually used as a weapon. First the shark uses its tail to herd a shoal of fish together. Then it thrashes its tail back and forth to stun as many fish as possible, knocking them unconscious before eating them up.

True to its name, the

RAGGED-TOOTH SHARK

does have an untidy mouthful of needle-like teeth. These almost seem to spill out of its jaws and can be seen even when the mouth is shut.

Despite their raggedy
appearance, these teeth are
ideal for grabbing smaller fish as well
as squid and other creatures.

With its unusual shape, the **SEAHORSE** might not look like a fish but it is. This fish feeds on minute sea creatures, which it sucks into its snout-like mouth. If you're close by, you can hear a 'pop' sound as it feeds!

The seahorse lies in wait for prey, holding on to a water plant with its prehensile (gripping) tail. When something comes within reach, the seahorse stretches out with the neck-like top part of its body, then strikes at the prey.

Perhaps the weirdest
thing about seahorses is that when the female
is pregnant, she transfers her tiny babies into
a pouch in the male's stomach, and he carries
them until they're old enough to emerge.

There are more than 30 different types of
seahorse, ranging in size from
1.5-35 centimetres long.

The extraordinary **ANGLERFISH** has a head that looks bigger than its body and a huge mouth filled with spiky teeth.

The female anglerfish has a special spine above its mouth, which acts like a fishing rod. The spine has a luminous tip that shines in the darkness of the deep sea and attracts other fish. They come close to see if this glowing morsel could be a tasty bit of food but then are engulfed by the anglerfish's huge mouth.

FAVOURITE FOODS

Chapter 7

Spiky sea urchins aren't everyone's idea of a good meal but they are one of the main foods of the

WOLF EEL.

With its big head, crunching teeth and elongated body, this creature is suited to its name, although it isn't a true eel but a kind of wolf fish. It grows to a maximum length of about 2.4 metres.

The wolf eel often curls itself into a hole or cave in the sea and waits with just its head sticking out for prey to come by.

It will also trawl the sea bed, looking for hard-bodied prey such as crabs and other shellfish as well as urchins, all of which it can crunch up with its strong jaws and fearsome teeth.

The

RED-BELLIED PIRANHA

lives in rivers in South America. Although only about 30 centimetres long, this fish is armed with extra-sharp, triangular-shaped, interlocking teeth and powerful jaws.

Most of the time piranhas prey on little fish, insects and other small creatures. But from time to time, a shoal of piranhas may find a wounded or struggling larger creature, such as a mammal that has fallen into the water. They can strip it to the bone in a feeding frenzy which can make the water appear to 'boil'. That's why piranhas have such a fearsome reputation.

TIGER SHARKS

are well known for being hungry hunters,
willing to eat more or less anything.
Fish, dolphins, other sharks and other marine
creatures, such as seals, are their usual diet.

Most measure about
3-4 metres long
but larger examples
have been known.

True to its namesake,
the tiger shark has dark
stripy markings on its body.

A tiger shark's teeth have serrated
edges and are so strong they can
even cut through turtle shells.

The **CANDIRU FISH**, which lives in rivers in the Amazon rainforest, is a parasite and feeds on the blood of other fish. The fish gets into the gills of larger fish where it lodges itself in place with the spines on its body. It then bites into an artery and quickly drinks up as much blood as it can.

Most candiru are only up to about 17 centimetres long, but there are some giant candiru. These awesome creatures actually bite straight into the gut of other fish.

The candiru has an excellent sense of smell and can detect any trace of blood in the water.

This tiny catfish has been known to swim right up the urethra of human beings who've been in the water and gone to the toilet. Because of the backwards-facing spines on the fish, they can only be removed by surgery. Don't panic though – this has only happened very occasionally.

The **ARCHERFISH**

feeds on small water creatures, but it also eats land-living insects. It has a very special way of catching them. When the fish spots prey on leaves overhanging the rivers where it lives, it spits out a jet of water to shoot them down. It aims with astonishing accuracy and can hit insects up to 1.2 metres away. The insects plop into the water and are swiftly swallowed by the archerfish.

BLACK GROUPERS are

often seen on coral reefs where they feed on smaller fish. These predators have an unusual family life. Most are born female, but some change to males once they have grown larger in order to reproduce.

Some sharks start their predatory
habits early – even before they are born!
Like many sharks, the female

RAGGED-TOOTH SHARK

has young that hatch from eggs and develop
inside her body. As they grow, the young sharks
feed on other eggs and even their siblings! After
9-12 months of development, only 2 pups are
born and they are up to 1 metre long. A full-
grown ragged-tooth shark is
3 metres long.

SALMON are fast-swimming predatory fish. They hatch in freshwater, but after a year or more travel to the ocean. Eventually they return to the river where they were born in order to spawn – lay and fertilize eggs.

The salmon make epic journeys in order to reach the right spot in the river, often leaping up waterfalls and swimming through rapids. It's believed they use ocean currents and variations in the Earth's magnetic field to navigate, and with a sense of smell more powerful than that of a bloodhound they can identify their birthplace by tracing the smell of the waters.

During the breeding season male salmon develop hooked jaws. When the males arrive at the spawning ground, they battle over territories.

The salmon do not feed during their migration. Most die after spawning, but a few return to the sea.

The female **ANGLERFISH** is an expert predator. But the male anglerfish, which is much smaller, does not need to hunt. Once a young male has found a female he attaches himself to her with his teeth. Eventually he becomes part of her body.

Both benefit. The male shares the female's bloodstream so does not need to find his own food. The female never has to look for a mate – which can be a difficult task in the dark depths of the ocean.

Become a detective with
The DEADLY Team

BBC EARTH

DEADLY
DETECTIVES
TOP TIPS TO TRACK WILDLIFE

STEVE
BACKSHALL

SPOT FASCINATING CLUES IN THE NATURAL WORLD . . .

The **GREEN MORAY EEL** is one of the largest morays and grows up to 2.5 metres long. It hunts at night, preying on creatures such as fish, crab, squid and shrimp.

The moray's eyesight is poor so it relies mostly on its excellent sense of smell for finding prey. It has 2 sets of nostrils, 1 set of which are at the end of the nose and look like little tubes. With these, the moray can pick up the tiniest scents from the water and then snap up prey with its pointed teeth.

The moray has no scales on its body but is covered with a coating of yellowish mucus, which helps to protect the skin.

It's hard to hide from a great white. The shark can sense the tiny electrical signals given off by muscular activities, such as the beating of a heart.

A **GREAT WHITE SHARK**
can pick up the scent of just
a drop of blood in the water
from a kilometre away.

BBC
EARTH

DEADLY 60

>>>>>>> **Factbook:**
Fish, Squid and Jellyfish

>>>>>>>>>

Orion
Children's Books

First published in Great Britain in 2013
by Orion Children's Books
This edition first published in 2014 by Orion Children's Books
a division of the Orion Publishing Group Ltd
Orion House
5 Upper St Martin's Lane
London WC2H 9EA
An Hachette UK Company

1 3 5 7 9 10 8 6 4 2

Copyright © The Orion Publishing Group Limited 2013
Derived from and based on the BBC TV series Deadly 60.

Photo credits
© BBC 2009: 18, 19, 30, 44, 45, 55, 68, 69; © BBC 2010: 8, 12, 26, 27, 34, 49, 52, 57, 58, 64,
65, 74; © BBC 2012: 2, 6, 9, 25, 28, 31, 32, 33, 38, 39, 40, 41, 46, 48, 50, 54; Brian Bevan: 72;
Helen Rushton: 60, 61; US National Oceanic and Atmospheric Administration: 62.
ARDEA: 1, 51 © Auscape; 14 © Mark Carwardine; 16 © Ken Lucas; 56 © Kurt Amler;
66 © M. Watson; 72 © Brian Bevan; 76 © Tom and Pat Leeson; 78 © Pat Morris.
SHUTTERSTOCK: 7, 24 © Ugo Montaldo; 21 © cynoclub.

Compiled by Jinny Johnson   Designed by Sue Michniewicz

A catalogue record for this book is available from the British Library.

ISBN 978 1 4440 1260 6

Printed and bound in China

MIX
Paper from
responsible sources
FSC® C008047
FSC
www.fsc.org

www.orionbooks.co.uk

CONTENTS

WHAT IS A FISH?

Fish were the first vertebrates – animals with backbones – and there are more kinds of fish than any other vertebrate. There are at least 30,000 species, living in the sea and in fresh water, and more are still being discovered.

GROUPER

TUNA

Fish breathe in water with
special structures called gills at
the sides of the head. As water flows
through the gills, oxygen is removed
and passes into the fish's blood.
Fish do not have legs, but they do
have fins and a tail to help them swim.

SHARK

There are two
main types of fish – cartilaginous
fish and bony fish. The cartilaginous
fish, such as sharks and rays, have
a skeleton made of a tough gristly
material called cartilage. Most
cartilaginous fish live in the sea.

Bony fish, the largest group of fish, have a skeleton made of bone. More than half of the species of bony fish live in the sea but there are plenty of freshwater fish too. Salmon, eel and tuna are all bony fish.

EEL

WHEN IS A FISH NOT A FISH?

Animals such as jellyfish and starfish are not fish at all but invertebrates – creatures without backbones. These and many other kinds of invertebrate animals, such as shrimp, squid, octopus and sea urchins, live in oceans, rivers and lakes.

JELLYFISH

BIGGEST
and SMALLEST

DEADLY

Chapter 1

The world's
largest fish is the

WHALE SHARK.

The biggest one ever known measured
13.5 metres – longer than a London bus –
and some may grow larger still.

Despite being so huge and having an enormous mouth, the whale shark eats only small fish and plankton (tiny animals that float in the water). It feeds by scooping up mouthfuls of sea water and filtering out the creatures.

The largest
predatory fish
in the ocean is the awesome

GREAT WHITE SHARK.

Some can grow to 6 metres long and weigh over
3,000 kilograms – more than 40 average humans.

A fast mover, the great white speeds through the
water at up to 24 kilometres an hour as it chases
prey such as fish, seals and even small whales.

A great white has
teeth that can be up
to 7.5 centimetres long
and have serrated edges like bread knives
– ideal for slicing through the flesh of prey.

ARAPAIMA

16

One of the biggest freshwater fish is the **ARAPAIMA**, also known as the pirarucu, which lives in South American rivers. This giant predator is up to 3 metres long and weighs 200 kilograms – as much as a lion.

Bigger still is the **MEKONG GIANT CATFISH** which can weigh 300 kilograms or more. This fish is not a predator and feeds only on water plants.

Cuttlefish are invertebrates – animals without backbones – and they are relatives of octopus and squid. Largest is the

GIANT CUTTLEFISH

which grows a metre or so long and weighs 10 kilograms.

Giant cuttlefish are masters of disguise. They can change colour to match their background when stalking prey and also according to their mood. Males become particularly brightly coloured in the breeding season in order to attract the attention of females.

Cuttlefish are expert hunters and snatch crabs and fish with a lightning-fast strike from their long tentacles. The tentacles are equipped with strong suckers for seizing prey.

Even bigger than the giant cuttlefish is its relative – the **GIANT SQUID**. This huge creature lives in the deep sea and has rarely been seen alive, but scientists think some can grow to an incredible 18 metres long – that's longer than 3 family cars parked in a line.

The **COLOSSAL SQUID** has an even larger, chunkier body and it's believed to have the biggest eyes of any animal. They may be as much as 27 centimetres across – the size of a basket ball.

The heaviest of all
bony fish (see pages
8-9) is the

OCEAN SUNFISH.

With its huge, almost circular body,
this fish looks like a swimming
head with fins and a frilly tail.
It can weigh 2,250 kilograms,
as much as a hippopotamus.

Jellyfish are the favourite food of this giant,
although it also eats small fish and plankton.

The world's smallest fish,

PAEDOCYPRIS PROGENETICA

reaches only 7.9 millimetres long as an adult – about the same size as a grain of rice. It's also the smallest known vertebrate. A member of the carp family, this little fish lives in swamps in Sumatra, Southeast Asia.

The smallest fish in European waters is the

GUILLET'S GOBY,

which is 24 millimetres long.

SPEED FREAKS

DEADLY

Chapter 2

TUNA are some of the fastest swimmers in the sea. These predatory fish can clock up speeds of 70 kilometres an hour. A tuna's body is beautifully streamlined – shaped like a torpedo so it can cut through the water with ease.

The **BLUEFIN TUNA** is one of the biggest of the group and weighs as much as 250 kilograms – more than 3 people. Bluefin tuna are thought to be able to swim across the Atlantic Ocean in less than 60 days.

Speedy over short distances is the
SAILFISH
which has a long upper jaw like a spear.
It moves at up to 110 kilometres an hour –
as fast as a speedboat. The fish gets
its name from the large sail-like fin on its
back. The biggest sailfish are over
3 metres long and weigh 50-100 kilograms.

The sailfish often attacks shoals of smaller fish,
such as sardines, herding them together, then
thrashing its long upper jaw from side to side to
stun them.

OCTOPUS are generally slow movers, dragging themselves along the sea bed with their arms. But, like their relatives, the squid, they have the ability to move fast by squirting water out of the siphon – a sort of water-jet propulsion.

Water flows into the body through an opening in the head. Muscles then squeeze the water out of a narrow tube at the back of the body to push the animal along. Squid and octopus can change the direction of the tube to propel themselves forwards or backwards.

STEVE FILMING WITH HUMBOLDT SQUID

Some squid can
travel at up to
40 kilometres an hour.

And one, the

HUMBOLDT or JUMBO SQUID,

can soar above the water surface and glide
for a short distance to avoid predators.

Not all sharks
are fast-movers. The

NURSE SHARK

spends most of its time moving slowly
around the sea bed, where it preys on shellfish
as well as fish and squid. This shark doesn't need
to move fast as it hunts in a different way to most
other sharks. Like a predatory vacuum cleaner,
it sucks up its prey with the help of an extra-large
pharynx (part of the throat).

VENOM

Chapter 3

Beautiful but ferocious, the

LIONFISH

has a boldly striped body and long
fan-like fins which it uses to trap prey
such as fish, shrimp and crabs.

The lionfish also has venom glands
at the base of the super-sharp spines
on its back. If attacked, the fish can
defend itself with these spines.

The **BLUE-RINGED OCTOPUS** is small but devastatingly deadly. At about 28 grams it weighs little more than a mouse, but it has a venomous bite that paralyses prey such as crabs and can even kill a person. It bites with its sharp parrot-like beak which is right in the middle of its 8 arms.

The **BOX JELLYFISH** is thought to be the most venomous animal on the planet and it kills more people in Australian waters than sharks and crocodiles. Its long tentacles are lined with thousands of stinging cells. When fired, these can kill prey in seconds and can even stop a human heart beating.

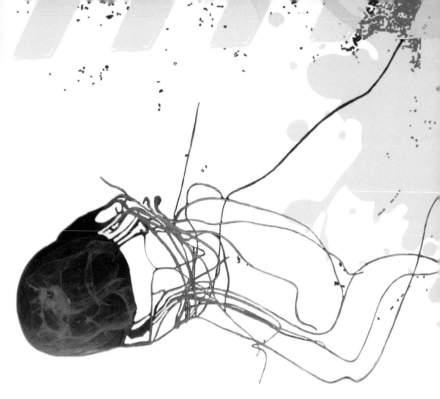

The stinging cells are not
triggered by touch but by the presence of
chemicals in the skin of the victim.

Like all jellyfish, the box jellyfish is not a fish
at all but a member of a group of invertebrates
called Cnidaria, which also includes corals
and sea anemones.

The CROWN-OF-THORNS STARFISH

lives on tropical coral reefs where it feeds on living coral and can cause great damage to the reef. It measures up to a metre across and has as many as 23 arms. The body and arms are covered with venomous spines, each 4–5 centimetres long, which protect it from attackers.

The crown of thorns' venom can cause severe pain and vomiting in humans.

Starfish have an unusual way of feeding. They throw their stomach lining out through their mouth and dissolve the prey with their digestive juices before sucking it into their body.

Each crown-of-thorns starfish can eat as much as 5 or 6 square metres of living coral every year.

SEA ANEMONES

might look like flowers
but they are predatory
animals that paralyse
prey with their venomous
tentacles.

The tentacles are arranged around the
sea anemone's mouth at the top of its pillar-like
body. If another animal brushes again a tentacle
the anemone fires out tiny stinging cells
and injects venom into the victim. It then
manoeuvres the prey into its mouth.

The biggest sea anemones can be as much
as 1.8 metres across, although most are
much smaller.

SUPER SENSES

DEADLY

Chapter 4